THE WHITE SOX
LITTLE BOOK OF

THE WHITE SOX FAN'S LITTLE BOOK OF WISDOM

Paul Whitfield

Taylor Trade Publishing
Lanham • New York • Dallas • Boulder • Toronto • Oxford

Published by Taylor Trade Publishing
An imprint of The Rowman & Littlefield Publishing Group, Inc.
4501 Forbes Boulevard, Suite 200
Lanham, Maryland 20706

Distributed by National Book Network

Library of Congress Cataloging-in-Publication Data
Whitfield, Paul, 1952–
    The White Sox fan's little book of wisdom / Paul Whitfield.—1st Taylor Trade Pub. ed.
        p. cm.
    ISBN 1-58979-126-6 (pbk. : alk. paper)
    1. Chicago White Sox (Baseball team)—History. 2. Baseball fans—Illinois—Chicago. I. Title.
    GV875.C58W43 2004
    796.357'64'0977311—dc22

                                                                                    2004003153

∞™ The paper used in this publication meets the minimum requirements of American National Standard for Information Sciences—Permanence of Paper for Printed Library Materials, ANSI/NISO Z39.48–1992.
Manufactured in the United States of America.

Doubleheader Dedication

To Kathleen McKernan,
friend, spouse,
and the AAA general manager's daughter
who helped me see that
the business side of baseball
is also a human side of baseball.

And to St. Rita,
the patron saint of ballplayers
and desperate cases,
which too often has described
the White Sox.

• Introduction •

White Sox baseball books are much rarer than tomes about the New York Yankees, the Boston Red Sox, or even the long-defunct Brooklyn Dodgers. Being a South Sider has never been especially popular or fashionable. The Yankees, Dodgers, and Red Sox have long claimed a national following, and their fans are every bit as ubiquitous as McDonald's, Starbucks, and Motel 6.

The White Sox have never pretended to have a national following. It is rare to meet a Sox fan beyond that narrow region of south Chicago and northwest Indiana. Among opinion makers, the ChiSox hardly have been worth a mention, unless it pertains to their mark of Cain—the selling of a World Series.

This is nothing new to White Sox fans. South Siders are accustomed to being treated as baseball's impoverished stepchild. The Sox seldom get respect even when they do win. In 1906, the underdog Sox stunned the baseball world and won the World Series. They took apart a 116-win Cubs team that looked as unsinkable as the *Titanic* would six years later. The baseball establishment never forgave the Sox for making their predictions look foolish, and even today baseball historians will dismiss the '06 Series as some oddity of nature that should never have occurred. In 1917, the Sox defeated the New York Giants in the World Series, but many people only remember the Giants' failure to cover home plate in a rundown. And of course the 1919 White Sox became the ultimate outsiders by bringing a longstanding gambling scandal—baseball's original sin—into the open.

Even in today's Chicago, the White Sox fan cannot escape that stray-dog status: No matter what the Sox do, it seems the Cubs will always be the city's pampered poodle.

If history were destiny, the White Sox fan would look at all this and declare himself the unluckiest fan on the face of the earth. But history doesn't tell the whole story. The fierce parochialness of the living Sox fan is stronger than the much-ballyhooed events, real or imagined, of baseball's past. In the neighborhood of White Sox baseball, the larger world holds no power. Local allegiances mean more. The Yankees, Dodgers, Red Sox, and to a lesser extent the Cubs have their well-known menus and the drive-through fans who show up in force when it is convenient. The ChiSox are more like that opposite phenomenon—the small, all-night diner with a clientele that is as workaday as a blue-plate special and is as strong as the coffee. And yes, there are still a few places on this planet where being a White Sox fan is the dominant form of life.

When I was a kid growing up in northern Indiana, I lived in such a place. Nearly every boy in my neighborhood was a White Sox fan. Some people don't believe me when I say that, because the Cubs have since brainwashed several generations of children into becoming Cubs fans, thanks to their superstation WGN. I have known men who went off to work daily, unaware that their sons and daughters were sitting in front of the TV watching the Cubs. Only when their children acquired the glazed look of Moonies and mumbled about the "Cubbies" at the supper table did these men realize what had happened. But in the late 1950s and early 1960s, kids were free to think for themselves. Naturally, they chose the White Sox over the Cubs.

Occasionally in that simpler era, you'd come across a Yankee fan in the neighborhood. Usually he was a loudmouthed kid who took pleasure in being obnoxious. On one level that was easy to understand: When those same loud-mouth kids sat in the moviehouse balcony watching World War II movies such as *The Longest Day*, they cheered for the Nazis. You see, the Nazis always opened an early lead, and Yankee fans love a winner above all else. But there was always a turning point in those war movies, when the Americans regained the advantage. Then the Yankee fans turned strangely silent, wishing they could cheer for the good guys, only it was too late to switch. That was how it was for Yankee fans in 1959 when their Nazi heroes crashed and the White Sox won the pennant.

In the neighborhood of my childhood, I only knew one Cubs fan. He was an odd kid who seldom came outside. Usually he stayed indoors and played the violin. When he did come out, he was wearing that blue cap and an odd, serial-killer smile. He had very pale skin and a squeaky voice. He was lousy at wiffle-ball but strangely enough he didn't seem to care.

On most summer days, we kids scarcely gave the Cubs a thought. The Cubs were like the Katzenjammer Kids, finding trouble in peculiar ways and losing even when it looked impossible. So what the Cubs were doing on a baseball diamond, unless it was especially comedic, didn't concern us. But on those rare days when this albino-looking kid came out with his Cubs cap on, we were baffled. To us, he was a human knuckleball.

You see, when the Cubs lost, he seemed to enjoy it. It was like he took pride in it.

Years later as an adult, I met many Cubs fans who on the surface appear almost normal. One should not be misled.

Loving a team because they lose in charming ways makes no more sense than the Yankee fans' loving a team because they win in evil ways.

Psychologists perhaps someday will unlock the mystery surrounding those North Siders. When they do, the Cubs fans can begin group therapy sessions at The Cell. They can learn to appreciate White Sox wonder ball—from Dummy Hoy and Fielder Jones to Shoeless Joe Jackson and Swede Risberg, from Ted Lyons and Luke Appling to Nellie Fox and Billy Pierce, from Dick Allen and Wilbur Wood to Harold Baines and Carlton Fisk, from Jack McDowell and Robin Ventura right up to Frank Thomas, Magglio Ordonez, and Paul Konerko.

This book is in recognition of that lost neighborhood of my childhood and all my White Sox pals. I know they are out there, and I know they do not have much use for the rest of the baseball world. Like the old neighborhood, this is a place to celebrate White Sox wonder ball, to despise the Darth Vader-like Yankees and to occasionally laugh at those Katzenjammer Cubs.

In more than a century of White Sox baseball, Sox fans have seen things move full circle several times—a first-place finish in their inaugural American

League season in 1901, followed by world, league or division titles in 1906, 1917, 1919, 1959, 1983, 1993, and Sox biggest offensive year, 2000. Both during and in between those wonder years, there were plenty of insufferable Yankee teams to cope with and frequently no shortage of comedy on the other side of Chicago.

But for the Sox fan winning, however rare, is the pleasure that surpasses all others. The White Sox fan lives for those all-too-brief days in first—the little moments when the ChiSox prevail and all is right with our small corner of the baseball world.

You're Only as Old as You Field and Hit

The first major-league Sox batter was the White Stockings' 1901 deaf-mute center fielder Dummy Hoy, who in that first AB hit a ground ball to first base for an easy out. Despite that forgettable start, Hoy had a fine season as the Sox's center fielder and leadoff man. He swiped 27 bases, legged out 11 triples, led the American League with 86 walks and was fourth in the league with 112 runs—all accomplished at the age of 39.

Sometimes Being
Byronic Is Moronic

The 1901 White Stockings were made in the image of Lord Byron—mad, bad, and dangerous to know. During that first season, shortstop Frank "Shugarts" Shugart was suspended for 23 games for getting in a fistfight with an umpire, and pitcher John "Katy" Katoll was suspended for 11 games after he beaned the same umpire in the leg during the fight.

3

The Ball May Be Dead But Don't Take That as an Excuse

In 137 games, the 1901 White Stockings produced 819 runs, a Dead Ball stunner of 5.98 runs per game. It was the highest run-production average for any team from 1901 through the last season of the Dead Ball era in 1920. Only two ChiSox teams have exceeded that average—field manager Jerry Manuel's 2000 White Sox with 6.04 runs per game, and Jimmy Dykes' 1936 White Sox with 6.01 runs per game.

Baby, You Were Born to Run

The 1901 White Stockings had the three top base stealers in the American League. Frank "Bald Eagle" Isbell led the league with 52 stolen bases; Sandow Mertes was second with 46; and Fielder Jones was third with 38. Only four other teams have done that—the 1930 Tigers, the 1949 Dodgers, and the 1957 and 1958 White Sox.

A Good Team Is Hard to Shut Out

The 1901 White Stockings suffered only two shutouts in a 136-game season. In the Dead Ball era, only two teams matched that or did better; the National League 1901 Pittsburgh Pirates were shut out only once and the American League 1902 Philadelphia Athletics were shut out twice. In more modern times, the 1977 South Side Hitmen were shut out just twice and the 2000 Sox were shut out only three times.

Remember, the Yankees Are the Real Bad Guys

"Then we forgot all about Al Capone, breweries, bribes and bullets as we watched (Ted) Lyons set the Yankees down. . . . Lyons twice struck out the mighty Babe Ruth."

—Eliot Ness with Oscar Fraley in the 1957 book *The Untouchables*

South Side Is South Side and North Side Is North Side

White Sox fans and Cubs fans are as different as night games and day games, as opposite as Dick Allen and Ernie Banks, as distant as the projects and the Gold Coast. A few famous fans:

White Sox Fan	Cubs Fan
Eliot Ness, mob buster	Bill Murray, ghostbuster
Nelson Algren, hard guy	George Will, hardly guy
Boss Daley, bear of a mayor	Jane Byrne, barely mayor
Harold Washington, he de man	Byrant Gumbel, he de mannequin

8

A Dime Short on Heroics Is Just Another Loss

With the Angels leading 10–4 and star closer Troy Percival coming in to pitch the ninth inning, Anaheim fans began to leave. It was August 11, 2003, and few people were paying much attention when Carlos Lee led off the inning with a single. Then Frank Thomas hit a home run and it was 10–6. Three sharply hit singles followed and it was 10–7. The home crowd was stirring uneasily now. Percival got Jose Valentin on a fly out to center but then hit Tony Graffanino with a pitch, loading the bases. Jamie Burke followed with a single and it was 10–8. With the bases still loaded, the Sox needed just one more hit for an unbelievable comeback. But Roberto Alomar struck out looking and Lee popped out to left field to end the game.

Lightning Can Strike the Same Place Far More Than Twice

In August 1906, the White Sox won 19 games in a row. It was the Dead Ball era's best win streak since the Providence Grays' 20-game streak in 1884. The Sox's streak became an American League record that would not be matched in the junior circuit until the Yankees won 19 straight in 1947. And it would not fall in the American League until the Oakland A's won 20 consecutive games in 2002.

10

You Don't Miss What You Never Had

In 1904, southpaw pitcher Doc White recorded five consecutive shutouts—a string that ended only when he pitched both ends of a doubleheader. The record stood 64 years until Dodger pitcher Don Drysdale broke it in 1968. When a sportswriter contacted the 89-year-old Doc White as Drysdale closed on his record, the reporter learned that the former pitcher didn't even know about the record. He had played in a simpler time.

The Last Shall Be First (If the Pitching Is Good Enough)

The 1906 White Sox won the pennant and a new nickname in the press—"the Hitless Wonders." They had gone 93–58 despite their last-place .230 batting average, their last-place .286 slugging average and their last-place home run total—seven. (There were five players in the American League who each hit more home runs than the entire Sox team.) The pitching staff, however, recorded 32 shutouts.

It's Bragging If You Can't Do It

Cubs left fielder Jimmy Sheckard predicted before the 1906 World Series that he would bat .400 against the highly regarded White Sox pitchers. The Cubs lost the Series to the Sox four games to two games and Jimmy Sheckard went 0 for 22.

Time Disguises Truth

The winner's share for the 1906 World Series was $1,874 per player. Losers each received $439.50. If that sounds like pocket lint for "exploited" ballplayers, keep this in mind: The average Chicago household in 1906 earned about $756 per year—thanks to a 60-hour-per-week job and the help of all who could work in a family of five.

Don't Work Any Harder Than You Must

In 1906, White Sox pitcher Nick Altrock won a game without throwing a single pitch. Altrock came into a tie game with two outs in the top of the ninth inning. His first move was a pickoff to first base, and it retired the side. When the Sox scored in the ninth, Altrock got the win even though he hadn't thrown a pitch to a single batter.

Self-Awareness Is Critical

"We stink. That's it. We stink."—outfielder Magglio Ordonez tries to explain on May 27, 2003, after the Sox dropped five games below .500, why a team with sluggers such as Frank Thomas, Ordonez, Carlos Lee, and Paul Konerko can't score runs.

Four Aces Don't Beat Every Hand

The 1920 Chicago White Sox had four 20-game winners—Red Faber, 23–13, Lefty Williams, 22–14, Dickie Kerr, 21–9, and Eddie Cicotte, 21–10—and still failed to catch the Cleveland Indians. (Five decades passed before a second team—the 1971 Baltimore Orioles—produced four 20-game winners. No other team in the American or National League has since produced four 20-game winners.)

Green Light Means Go, Yellow Means Go Like Hell

In 1912, Sox second baseman Eddie "Cocky" Collins
twice stole six bases in a game.

18

There's No Prize for Being the Best at Overlooked Virtues

From 1983 to 1987, Harold Baines was the most consistent pressure hitter in all of baseball. He was the only player to bat above .320 with runners on base in each of those five seasons. And he was the only major league player to hit over .280 with 20 or more home runs in each of those seasons. Yet Baines never won a batting title, never won MVP, and never led the league in RBIs, runs or home runs.

Finishing What You Start Is the Main Idea

Billy Pierce is the only White Sox pitcher to lead or share the lead in American League complete games for three consecutive seasons. Pierce notched 21 complete games in 1956, 16 the following year and 19 in 1958.

20

A Chip on Your Shoulder Needn't Be a Problem

In 1972, Dick Allen brought his reputation for troublemaking to Chicago and naturally was embraced by all those South Side fans who carry chips on their own shoulders. Allen's bat lifted a mediocre team into contention, boosted attendance 41 percent and saved the franchise from being relocated. The Sox were in first place as late as August 28 and Allen drove in 113 runs, which was 19.9 percent of the team's total. No other Sox player before or after has driven in a greater percentage of his team's runs—not Albert Belle in 1998 (17.6 percent of the runs), not Frank Thomas in 1993 (16.5 percent), no one.

There's Never a Crowd at the Top of the Mountain

Frank Thomas became the third player in baseball history to record at least 20 HRs, 100 runs, 100 RBIs and 100 walks in four consecutive seasons in 1991–1994. He joined Ted Williams and Lou Gehrig as the only players to do it. (In 1998, Barry Bonds became the fourth player to do it.)

Kenny, We Hardly Knew Ye

Baseball's amateur draft was launched in 1965 and the White Sox had the 17th first-round pick. Johnny Bench, Nolan Ryan, Sal Bando, Hal McRae, Gene Tenace, and Graig Nettles were still available. The Sox snubbed them all for Ken Plesha, a catcher from the University of Notre Dame. Plesha rewarded the Sox by batting .186 in a four-year minor league career.

Go for It

Brian Downing's first big-league hit came as a White Sox in 1973.
It was an inside-the-park home run.

Owners Can Be Idiots

On July 29, 1997, the White Sox were only four and a half games behind the first-place Cleveland Indians when owner Jerry Reinsdorf threw in the towel and sent Harold Baines, who was batting .305, to the Baltimore Orioles for cash. Two days later, with the Sox three and a half games out, Reinsdorf declared that the team could not possibly win the division and traded away three more veterans—Wilson Alvarez, Danny Darwin, and Roberto Hernandez—for six minor leaguers, Mike Caruso, Brian Manning, Lorenzo Barcelo, Keith Foulke, Bob Howry, and Ken Vining. The Sox sagged to an 80–81 finish, six games back.

The Little Dog Bites

Second baseman Nellie Fox was the toughest Sox to strike out. Eleven times Fox led the American League in fewest strikeouts. In 1958, Fox went 98 consecutive games without whiffing. Hall of Fame pitcher Bob Feller listed Fox as one of the four toughest outs he ever faced.

Breaking Up Is Easy to Do

A baseball career spent with one team is a rarity. Catcher Ray Schalk spent his whole career in a White Sox uniform—then in 1929 played his final five games for the New York Giants. Big Ed Walsh pitched 13 seasons for the Sox—then tossed his last 18 innings in a Boston Braves uniform. But three Sox players had long careers without playing for any other team:

Ted Lyons, pitcher, 21 seasons
Luke Appling, shortstop, 20 seasons
Red Faber, pitcher, 20 seasons

The Best-Laid Plans Lead to Third Place

"The Sox are too proud to take anyone's leavings. If we cannot be first, we care not for second, which is but the anteroom to oblivion. Ever notice the man who plays second fiddle in the orchestra? What does he amount to? He is a bald-headed little galoot who makes the same motions for 25 years. The first fiddle is in the public eye, and that is where the Sox will be. Second place be blowed."

—Player-manager Fielder Jones to a sportswriter in September 1907. (The Sox finished the season in third place.)

Above All, Think Small

"I can't tell you how many fans come up to me and say, 'No matter what you do, beat the Cubs.' I ask them, 'Wouldn't you rather have us win the division?' You'd be surprised how many say no."
—Sox field manager Tony LaRussa in 1986

Being the Best Won't Excuse Dishonesty

In the three seasons sandwiched around World War I (1916, 1917, and 1919), the Chicago White Sox won more games than anybody in baseball, captured two pennants and a World Series, but are remembered only for throwing the 1919 World Series.

1. Sox 284–164 or .634 winning percentage
2. N.Y. Giants 271–177 or .605
3. Cleveland Indians 270–177 or .604
4. Cincinnati Reds 256–191 or .573
5. N.Y. Yankees 246–200 or .552

Don't Push Your Luck

On June 12, 2003, Sox pitcher Bartolo Colon struck out the San Francisco Giants' Barry Bonds in each of his first three at bats. Bonds came up a fourth time in the ninth inning with a runner on first and the Sox leading 4–2. Field manager Jerry Manuel decided to stick with Colon. "He had challenged all night and won," said Manuel. Bonds tied the game with a home run and San Francisco went on to win, 8–4.

The Path to Damnation Begins with a Beach Ball

Four things true White Sox fans
don't even think about doing in their park:
1. Toss a beach ball around in the stands.
2. Watch the Bears on a portable TV.
3. Throw an opponent's home run back on the field.
4. Jump to their feet for a warning-track fly ball.

Curses That End on Time
Have More Credibility

After the 1962 season, when Luis Aparicio's pay was slashed and then he was traded, a bitter Aparicio said the White Sox would not win a pennant for 40 years. Aparicio, who was on the 1959 pennant-winning team, was destined to become a Hall of Fame shortstop, and the Sox were destined to make the Aparicio curse come true. The White Sox have been in the playoffs three times since '59—in 1983, 1993, and 2000—and have fallen short of a pennant each time. (The curse should have expired after 1999, but the Sox kept losing anyhow.)

Enjoy It for Tomorrow
It May Be Gone

In 1916, the White Sox become the first Chicago team to draw 40,000 fans. But that was then and this is now: The Sox have not outdrawn the Cubs since 1992.

'Do No Harm'
Isn't the Front Office Way

In February 1929, White Sox outfielder Bibb Falk was sent to
Cleveland for backup catcher Martin Autry. Falk had the best slugging
percentage of his career in 1929 (.502) while Autry batted .228 over
two seasons of part-time duty.

Beauty Is Truth and Truth Is Beauty, But Poetry Seldom Wins Pennants

White Sox fans understand that there are few things more beautiful than a center fielder running down a "sure double" to give it a decent burial in his mitt. The White Sox have tied or led the American League in fielding average 21 times—1902, 1904, 1905, 1907, 1908, 1909, 1922, 1926, 1927, 1952, 1953, 1954, 1955, 1956, 1957, 1959, 1960, 1961, 1962, 1984, 1985—yet only one of those teams won the pennant.

'If Only' Has No Place in History

If only Babe Ruth had faced White Sox pitching every day in 1927, he never would have hit 60 home runs. The White Sox gave up just six home runs to the Babe in 1927—the fewest of any team he faced. (Three of the Sox gopher balls came off Tommy Thomas while Sarge Connally, Ted Blankenship, and Ted Lyons each gave up one home run to Ruth.)

Blame Is Rarely Divided Fairly

Boston Red Sox pitcher Tracy Stallard gets the blame for giving up home run No. 61 to Roger Maris, but the White Sox deserved the greater portion of blame. In 1961, Sox pitchers gave up more gopher balls to Maris than any other team. Maris hit 13 home runs off the ChiSox. Billy Pierce, Cal McLish, and Russ Kemmerer gave up 2 home runs each, and Bob Shaw, Early Wynn, Ray Herbert, Frank Baumann, Don Larsen, Warren Hacker, and Juan Pizarro each yielded 1 home run.

38

Last Hurrahs Are Nice But Scoring Runs Is Even Better

In old Comiskey Park's last season, the 1990 White Sox, under field manager Jeff Torborg, became the only Sox team never to be shut out at home. The Sox finished in second place at 94–68.

Great Accomplishments Come in Threes

Lance "One Dawg" Johnson became the first player to lead or share the league lead in triples for four consecutive seasons. In 1991, Johnson tied Paul Molitor for the league lead with 13 triples. He led the AL with 12 triples in 1992, with 14 triples in 1993, and with 14 triples in 1994. In 1995, he lost the American League lead in triples to Kenny Lofton by one triple.

You Can Hear the Sound of One Hand Clapping at the Ballpark

Sometimes when the sun dwelt at old Comiskey Park, you could look through the open arches and see the trees trembling in the breeze, and as the players trotted out to the field in between innings, the park became oddly quiet. The only thing you heard was that vague, restless noise made when fans aren't focused on anything—the nothing sounds of a slow game. Like Indian burial grounds, baseball parks are sacred turf. In the small children who sit in the stands with their mitts on, who dream casually of a life in baseball as if it were as easy as buying a comic book, in those children, an old man can see the buried child of his past.

Sometimes a Dream Is Just a Dream

In 1956, Robert Leroy Powell appeared on a Topps baseball card with this promise printed on the back: "The Chisox feel that Bob will be a big league star." Powell appeared in two games, scored a run, but never recorded an at bat.

Good Things Happen

The White Sox's most consistent streak of winning seasons was from 1951 to 1967. During that period, the ChiSox had winning seasons for 17 consecutive years. (Only two teams have had longer runs of good fortune—the Yankees, who had 39 winning seasons in a row from 1926 to 1964, and the Baltimore Orioles, who had 18 consecutive winning seasons from 1968 to 1985.)

Rodney Dangerfield Could Have Played on the Sox

"We don't get as much respect as the North Side does. What better time to do it?"—Jose Valentin on June 27, 2003, after hitting a home run in the bottom of the ninth inning for a 4–3 White Sox win over the Cubs.

Sin Has a Rather Lackluster Payoff

Shoeless Joe Jackson, kicked out of baseball at 31 after the Black Sox scandal, operated a dry cleaning business and later ran a liquor store. Fred McMullins, banned at 28, went into law enforcement. Buck Weaver, out of baseball at 30, worked at a racetrack window and in a drugstore. Lefty Williams, gone at 27, managed a garden-nursery business. Happy Felsch, banned at 29, opened a tavern. Eddie Cicotte, out at 36, took up farming and later worked as a game warden. Swede Risberg, out at 25, worked a dairy farm and later opened a saloon on the Oregon-California border. Chick Gandhil, who organized the bribe-taking, was done at 32 and became a plumber.

False Hopes
Are No Match for Reality

The White Sox won 13 games in a row in 1908; 11 consecutive games in 1915; 14 straight games in 1951; and 12 in a row in 1961. In none of those seasons did the Sox finish first.

Always Pick Up
Where You Left Off

In 1993, White Sox pitcher Wilson Alvarez won his final
seven decisions and then began the next season by winning
his first eight decisions.

Facing Up to Your Shortcomings Is Painful

In 1970, Sox third baseman Bill Melton lost a pop-up in the lights in Baltimore and got hit in the face with the ball.

The South Side Is No Place for Tourists

"Fans come to Comiskey Park to watch the game. They appreciate good baseball, and when you don't play good baseball, they'll let you know about that, too. But most people go to Wrigley Field to see how many bars they can hit before and after the game. Wrigley Field is more of a tourist attraction than anything else."
—First baseman Paul Konerko in 2001.

Be Grateful for Small Favors

Floyd "The Blotter" Baker, who played for the White Sox for seven seasons, was the fourth worst home-run hitter in live-ball history. He had 2,280 career at bats, but hit only one home run. That sole home run was hit in 1949 while he was playing for the White Sox.

Being First Is No Guarantee You Will Be Remembered

In 1977, the White Sox's Mary Shane became the
first woman baseball radio broadcaster.

A Masterful Performance Doesn't Necessarily Get You the Job

Charlie Lindstrom appeared in one game as a White Sox catcher in 1958. He drew a walk, hit a triple, scored and drove in a run, recorded two putouts, and never played another major league game. He remains forever perfect with a 1.000 batting average, a 1.000 fielding average, and an awesome 3.000 slugging percentage.

Sometimes You Win
without Deserving It . . .

On May 9, 1901, Cleveland Blues pitcher Earl Moore held the White
Stockings hitless for nine innings, but lost in the 10th inning, 4–2,
when Chicago got two hits. It was the American League's first
nine-inning no-hitter.

53

But If You're Playing the Yankees, You Always Deserve It

On July 1, 1990, New York Yankee pitcher Andy Hawkins pitched an eight-inning no-hitter at old Comiskey Park and lost to the White Sox, 4–0. Here's how it happened: With the score 0–0 and two outs in the bottom of the eighth, Sammy Sosa got on base on a Yankee error and then stole second base. Hawkins walked Ozzie Guillen and Lance Johnson to load the bases. Yankee left fielder Jim Leyritz then dropped Robin Ventura's fly ball and three runs scored. Yankee right fielder Jesse Barfield then dropped a fly ball hit by Ivan Calderon and Ventura scored. Hawkins got Dan Pasqua to pop out to the shortstop for the third out. The Yankees failed to score in the top of the ninth and the game ended without a Sox hit.

54

The Thing You Desire May Be Right in Front of You

After winning the pennant in 1959, the White Sox traded three rookies away in a search for power hitting. The three were Johnny Callison, who had hit four home runs for the Sox and had 222 career home runs ahead of him; Norm Cash, who had hit four home runs for the Sox and had 373 additional career home runs to come; and Johnny Romano, who had hit five home runs for the Sox and had 124 more in his future. In return for the rookies, who had 719 home runs ahead of them, the Sox got Gene Freese, Minnie Minoso, and Dick Brown, who together had 148 home runs left in their careers, only 54 of which they produced for the White Sox.

It Helps If You Spell Things Out

In July 2001, as part of the James Baldwin trade to the Dodgers, Sox general manager Ken Williams asked Los Angeles to throw in "Berry." The Dodgers agreed to send the Sox "Barry." And so, instead of 23-year-old minor league pitcher Jonathan Berry, Chicago found itself with Jeff Barry, a 32-year-old minor league outfielder.

When Mom Says One Thing and Your Heart Says Another, Go with the Heart

The White Sox manager with the highest win percentage—Fielder Jones, 426–293, .592—gave up baseball after the 1908 season, as his mother had nagged him to do, and entered the timber business. It didn't last, and Jones eventually returned to baseball, coaching Oregon Agricultural College to its first and only Northwest Championship. Two years later, he returned to the big leagues to manage the St. Louis Federals and the St. Louis Browns.

True Fame Is Found on the Comics Page

Ollie Bejma, second baseman for the 1939 White Sox, became famous on the comics page 35 years after he was out of baseball. Charles Schulz, the creator of "Peanuts," had Snoopy mention Bejma in a 1974 comic strip. Snoopy called Bejma a shortstop but he actually was a second baseman. Bejma played in 90 games for the Sox in 1939, batting .251 and hitting eight home runs in 307 at bats.

Sometimes No Matter How Well You Play, It's Not Enough

On Sept. 22, 1964, the White Sox were three and a half games behind the Yankees with 9 games left for the Sox and 12 games left for the Yankees. The Sox won all 9 games while the Yankees won 8 of 12— just enough to finish one game ahead of the Sox.

Some Performances Are Long Running

In 1999, second baseman Ray Durham became the first White Sox to steal 30 or more bases in four straight seasons since shortstop Luis Aparicio did it in 1959–1962. (Of course, Aparicio also did it for two additional seasons after he was traded.)

'Might Have Beens' Are Forever

At 26, catcher Ray Shook appeared in one game for the 1916
White Sox. Like Moonlight Graham, he never got an at bat,
putout, or second chance. After baseball, he moved to Indiana
and started a trucking company. He died in South Bend, Indiana,
on September 16, 1970.

61

Persistence Pays

Kid Willson came up to the big leagues in 1918, the year five White Sox starters were missing due to World War I. The 22-year-old outfielder was hitless in four games. When Shoeless Joe Jackson and Happy Felsch returned, there was no room for Willson. For eight years, Kid Willson did not play another major league game. Then in 1927, he returned to the show. In seven games with the Sox, he recorded six putouts, got 10 at bats and . . . one single! He left the Sox and the majors forever after that '27 season, but Kid Willson had gotten his hit.

Divine Justice Is Never Far Off

After the Black Sox World Series betrayal of 1919, the White Sox spent 40 seasons wandering in the desert of second place, seventh place, fifth place, eighth place, sixth place, third place, fourth place, every place and any place but first place. It is not lost on White Sox fans that the South Siders spent exactly as much time looking for their next pennant as Moses did looking for the Promised Land. Theologically, the Sox fan knows that has to mean something.

63

Moses Never Made It to the Promised Land (He Moved to Baltimore)

Field manager Paul Richards was the Moses who prepared the White Sox for their great comeback in 1959. Richards, faced with the Pharaoh-like Yankees, brought sharp fielding, good pitching, and 1906-style, go-go "small ball" back to Chicago. For the first time since the Shoeless Joe years, the White Sox finished above .500 three seasons in a row. Like Moses, Richards never saw the Promised Land—at least, not in Chicago. He departed for Baltimore without seeing a pennant flag flying on the South Side.

Location Is Everything

During the Al Lopez era from 1957 to 1965, the White Sox won more games than any team in the National League. In those nine years, the record looked like this:

White Sox, 811–615, .569

Dodgers, 792–631, .557

Braves, 788–632, .555

The Dodgers won three pennants and the Braves two pennants while the Sox won only one pennant because they were in the American League (Yankees, 851–574, .597, seven pennants).

There Are No Support Groups in the Clubhouse

Frank Isbell, infielder for the Sox for nine seasons in the Dead Ball era, was so uncomfortable with his baldness that he refused to have his photograph taken without his cap on. His teammates responded by giving him the nickname, "Bald Eagle."

66

Coffee Is Better When It's Fresh

A "cup of coffee" is slang for a few games in the big leagues. Often it is said of rookies who come up in late September. But the White Sox often serve cups of coffee to once-great players who are on their way out.

1922 Johnny Evers, 1 game
1925 Chief Bender, 1 inning
1961 Don Larsen, 7 wins
1974 Ron Santo, 5 homers
1982 Sparky Lyle, 11 games
1986 Steve Carlton, 4 wins

Sometimes You Get the Dream, Sometimes You Get the Nightmare

In 1916, Ceylon Wright played in eight games as a White Sox shortstop and went 0 for 18. He committed five errors and struck out seven times. His sole offensive accomplishment was drawing a walk. He never played again for the White Sox or any other major league team.

68

It Takes a Village to Raise a Pennant Flag

In 1908, right-hand pitcher Ed Walsh led the American League in seven categories: winning percentage (.727), wins (40), strikeouts (269), complete games (42), shutouts (11), saves (6), and innings pitched (464). Despite a rare, league-dominating performance (only Christy Mathewson, Walter Johnson, and Grover Alexander had seven-category seasons in the Dead Ball era), Walsh could not carry the Sox to the pennant. Chicago finished in third place, a game and a half out.

Don't Ask for Whom the Bell Tolls

In March 1992, White Sox outfielder Sammy Sosa (28 home runs in three South Side seasons) was traded to the Cubs for George Bell. Two seasons later, Bell was out of baseball after hitting a total of 38 home runs and batting .240 over his last two years with the Sox. Sosa went on to break Roger Maris' home run mark and hit more than 500 home runs for the Cubs.

Success Dismisses the Odds

In 1924, White Sox pitcher Sloppy Thurston won 20 games for the last place ChiSox. Thurston was 20–14 with a league-leading 28 complete games. The Sox were 46–73 when Sloppy wasn't involved in the decision.

Being a Cover Story Is Bad Luck

On March 19, 1979, *Sports Illustrated* put Sox rookie shortstop Harry Chappas—5-foot-3, 150 pounds—on its cover. The 21-year-old kid was the Sox's Opening Day shortstop and batted .288 in 26 games, but committed seven errors and was sent down. He returned to the show in 1980 for another 26 games and this time made only one error, but he batted .160 and never played in the majors again.

Sentiments Have Value

In December 1970, the White Sox sent future Hall of Fame shortstop
Luis Aparicio to Boston for second baseman Mike Andrews and
shortstop Luis Alvarado. A season later, the Sox were contenders and
needed a veteran shortstop. Aparicio deserved to finish his career as a
White Sox and at 38 he could still hit (.257 in 1972) and field.
Meanwhile, Alvarado (batting .213) split shortstop duties with Rich
Morales (batting .206) and Mike Andrews batted .220.

Sometimes Too Good to Be True Is True

On September 11, 1931, playing against the White Sox,
Babe Ruth hit into a triple play.

Even Legends Have Bad Days

On August 31, 1914, White Sox first baseman Jack Fournier
hit two home runs off Walter Johnson.

Respect the Elderly (They May Be Carrying a Big Bat)

In 1936, shortstop Luke Appling batted .388—the highest average ever for a shortstop. But Appling's most remarkable accomplishment came 32 years after he was out of baseball. On July 19, 1982, at the age of 75, Appling hit a 250-foot home run off Warren Spahn at the Cracker Jack Old Timers' Game at Washington's RFK Stadium.

That Junk in the Garage
May Be an Antique

In May 1956, the White Sox picked up reliever Gerry Staley on
waivers from the Yankees. Staley appeared in a league-leading 67
games for the 1959 Sox, sporting a 2.24 ERA. In June 1958, the Sox
got Turk Lown from Cincinnati for the waiver price. Lown led the
league in relief wins and saves in 1959. He appeared in 60 games,
recording 9 wins and 15 saves with a 2.89 ERA.

77

Never Confuse a Fast Start and the Long Run

In 1973, the White Sox opened the first two months of the season 27–15, including a nine-game win streak. They were in first place with a three-game lead over Minnesota and a six-game lead over the previous season's World Champion Oakland A's. But the hopes raised were about to be cruelly dashed. The Sox played .417 ball the rest of the season, going 50–70 and finishing in fifth place, 17 games behind the A's.

There Are Second Acts on the South Side

In 1931, Ted Lyons was 30 years old and had more than 120 wins behind him when he injured his arm. With Lyons' fastball lost, Sox manager Donie Bush thought the right-hander was finished. Lyons won only four games that season. But Lyons developed a knuckleball and came back to play for 12 more seasons. He retired with 260 career wins despite missing three seasons as a Marine in World War II.

Play the Game the Right Way

On May 22, 1990, Yankees outfielder "Neon" Deion Sanders hit a pop-up toward the shortstop, ran partway to first and then quit running. White Sox catcher Carlton Fisk yelled at Sanders to run the ball out. "Yankee pinstripes, Yankee pride. I'm playing for the other team and it offended me," Fisk said later.

The Right Place at the Right Time Always Helps

On May 9, 1984, White Sox pitcher Tom Seaver got two wins in one day. The first game was a continuation of what turned out to be a 25-inning duel that had begun the day before. Seaver entered the game as a reliever when the Sox bullpen was depleted; he got the win when Harold Baines hit a home run to finish the eight-hour-and-six-minute game. Seaver started the second game and pitched 8 1/3 innings for his second win.

For Some People, the Game Just Goes On and On

After a career that ran from 1949 to 1964, 53-year-old Minnie Minoso appeared in three games for the Sox in 1976, getting a single in eight at bats. Four years later, he appeared in two games, going 0 for 2. In 1993, two years after the commissioner of baseball ruled he could not be activated again, the 70-year-old Minoso came to bat as the designated hitter for the St. Paul Saints against Thunder Bay in the independent Northern League. He grounded out to the pitcher. In 2003, Minoso again appeared as the DH for the Saints against the Gary Steelheads. He drew a base on balls.

82

A Peak Never Seems Like a Peak While You're There

In 1983, LaMarr Hoyt won 24 games and Richard Dotson won 22 for the White Sox, leading the ChiSox to a division title. It was the most wins by two teammates since the 1970 Orioles, but neither Hoyt nor Dotson ever won 20 games in a season again. Dotson struggled with injuries and Hoyt eventually ended up serving time in prison on a narcotics conviction. Both were out of baseball before they were 32 years old.

83

Power Outages
Follow Power Surges

For the first time in Sox history, the ChiSox had the American League's No. 1 and No. 2 home-run-percentage hitters in 1983—Ron Kittle at 6.7 percent and Greg Luzinski at 6.4 percent. No team had done that since Baltimore's Frank Robinson and Boog Powell in 1966. The two Sox hit 67 home runs together with slugging averages of .504 and .502. The following season Kittle's slugging average dropped to .453, Luzinski's fell to .364, and the pair hit only 45 home runs.

We're Due

"I think we're the only team in baseball that hasn't gotten on a roll. We're due." —Field manager Jerry Manuel in June 2003 with the White Sox at 30–36 and still waiting for a win streak. The streak came a month later when the White Sox won 13 of 14 games and moved into first place.

Bad Starts Are Painful for Everybody

Sox knuckleball pitcher Wilbur Wood tied a major league record when he beaned three batters in the first inning on September 10, 1977. The Sox lost to the Angels, 6–1.

Pick Your Fights Carefully

After a pitch from Nolan Ryan struck Sox third baseman Robin
Ventura on August 4, 1993, Ventura charged the mound. The 46-year-
old Texan waited for the 26-year-old Ventura, grabbed him in a
headlock and punched him six times. The "box" score: Ventura hit
by a pitch, thoroughly whipped before 32,312 fans, suspended
for two games, and oh yes, the White Sox lost, 5–2. No action
was taken against Ryan.

Glory Days Are Too Brief

By mid-June 2000, White Sox pitcher James Baldwin was 10–1 with a 3.11 ERA. In July, he was an American League all-star selection and got the win as the National League fell to the junior circuit, 6–3. But Baldwin's glory days in 2000 were brief. For the rest of the season, he went 4–6 with a 6.21 ERA.

Congratulations Rides the Bus

"Here I just get my congratulations from my teammates." —Sox shortstop Jose Valentin on April 27, 2000, after hitting a single, a double, a triple, and a home run in Comiskey Park. Valentin had spent eight seasons without achieving that feat in Milwaukee—where a player gets a Harley-Davidson motorcycle for "hitting for the cycle."

89

Seven Runs Cover
a Multitude of Errors

On April 3, 2000, Jose Valentin committed four errors in one game
against the Oakland A's. The White Sox won anyway, 7–3.

No Lead Is Safe

On June 18, 1911, at Detroit's Bennett Field, the White Sox jumped off to a 13–1 lead after five and a half innings. The Sox ended up losing 16–15 as Ty Cobb led the Tiger comeback with five hits and five RBIs.

91

A Dumb Move Is Sometimes Followed by a Dumber Move

On August 2, 1985, New York Yankee Rickey Henderson came up to bat in the seventh inning with Bobby Meacham on second base and Dale Berra on first base. Henderson hit a single to left-center and Meacham decided to try to score. Incredibly, Berra also decided to go for home. Ozzie Guillen fired the relay to Carlton Fisk, who tagged out Meacham and then Berra, who was only a few steps behind. The White Sox won, 6–5.

Be Aware of Significant Obstacles

In game two of the 1917 World Series, White Sox pitcher Red Faber
tried to steal third base. Imagine teammate Buck Weaver's surprise:
Weaver already was standing on third base! Faber was tagged out, but
the Sox beat the Giants anyhow, 7–2.

Even Champions Stumble

The 1917 World Champion White Sox led the American League in
runs, triples, and stolen bases. But amazingly, they were the victims of
no-hitters on two consecutive days. St. Louis Browns pitcher Ernie
Koob held the Sox hitless on May 5, and the next day in the second
game of a doubleheader, the Browns' Bob Groom held the Sox hitless.
The Sox then woke up and won 19 of their next 22 games.

94

Rage, Rage Against the Dying of the Light

Johnny Dickshot, a substitute outfielder for several seasons in the National League, became an everyday player for the White Sox in 1945 at the age of 35. That season the left fielder's .302 batting average was third best in the American League, and he finished fourth in triples with 10 and fifth in stolen bases with 18. After the season, the White Sox released him and he never played in the big leagues again.

Luck Is Part of the Game

"Baseball is a lucky game. I'm lucky that I got my first grand slam today, the first one of my career." —Miguel Olivo on June 20, 2003, after hitting a home run with the bases loaded against the Cubs. And Olivo was lucky. The batter before him walked on a checked swing with two strikes and two outs. Some observers thought he went around for the third out, but the umpire said no. Olivo got his at bat and his grand slam, and the Sox won, 12–3.

There Are Those Who Never Learn

In 1954, Sox catcher Sherman Lollar threw out
18 would-be base stealers in a row.

Be Unforgettable

On May 7, 1999, rookie Carlos Lee became the first Sox player
to hit a home run in his very first major league at bat.
The White Sox beat Oakland, 7–1.

98

Despair and Hope
Are Next-Door Neighbors

Toronto's Dave Stieb had a no-hitter and a 6–0 lead against the White Sox through eight innings on August 24, 1985. In the top of the ninth, Rudy Law ended the no-hit bid with a home run. Bryan Little was next to bat and he hit a home run. Stieb was pulled and reliever Gary Lavelle came in to pitch. Harold Baines was the first batter he faced, and Baines hit a home run. The Blue Jays then brought in their ace reliever Tom Henke and he finished the inning to preserve the win.

Living the Dream
Doesn't Guarantee Victory

On July 6, 1999, rookie center fielder Chris Singleton went 5 for 6
against Kansas City, hitting for the cycle with two singles, a double, a
triple, and a home run. Singleton drove in four runs and scored three.
But the White Sox lost the game, 8–7, in the 10th inning when
reliever Keith Foulke gave up three hits and a run.

The Short End of History Is the Worst Place to Be

On May 10, 2002, the destined-to-be-world-champion Anaheim Angels pounded the White Sox 19–0. It was the Sox's worst loss ever.

Be Worthy of Winning

"We have to go one game at a time, one inning at a time, one out at a time, and not worry about who's coming and who's going. You have to stare it in the face—because if you don't, how will you be worthy of a championship? The championship teams I've been a part of have been able to do that—and if you don't, you're not worthy of a championship." —Jerry Manuel on June 13, 2003. Three months later, the Sox collapsed, losing five straight to the Twins.

About the Author

Paul Whitfield was born and raised in South Bend, Indiana, and is currently serving a life sentence as a Chicago White Sox fan. A journalist at *Investor's Business Daily*, he now lives in Culver City, California, with his wife, Kathleen, who is a Boston Red Sox fan and the daughter of the former AAA Albuquerque Dukes general manager and former Eastern League president, the late Pat McKernan. A shared hatred of the Yankees is the common ground in their mixed baseball marriage. They have four children who are being raised as ChiSox fans, though one daughter already has declared some affection for the Yankees. Whitfield is a member of the Society for American Baseball Research and is also the keeper of www.thesouthsider.com, a Web site for White Sox fans.